BRITAIN'S CENTURY
A PICTORIAL HISTORY

Press Association

BRITAIN'S CENTURY

A PICTORIAL HISTORY

MAINSTREAM
PUBLISHING

EDINBURGH AND LONDON

First published in Great Britain in 1999 by
MAINSTREAM PUBLISHING COMPANY (EDINBURGH) LTD
7 Albany Street
Edinburgh EH1 3UG

ISBN 1 84018 256 3

A catalogue record for this book is available from the British Library

Designed by Janene Reid
Typeset in Gill Sans Light
Printed and bound in Great Britain by Butler & Tanner Ltd

Dan Gumbrell, a typical old English farmer, lighting his pipe, 1900.

Winston Churchill, portrait taken when he joined the Liberals in 1904.

Emmeline Pankhurst (second right) with her daughter Christabel and other suffragette leaders at a meeting at Clements Inn, 1908.

Suffragette housemaid, 1908, during the campaign for the enfranchisement of women.

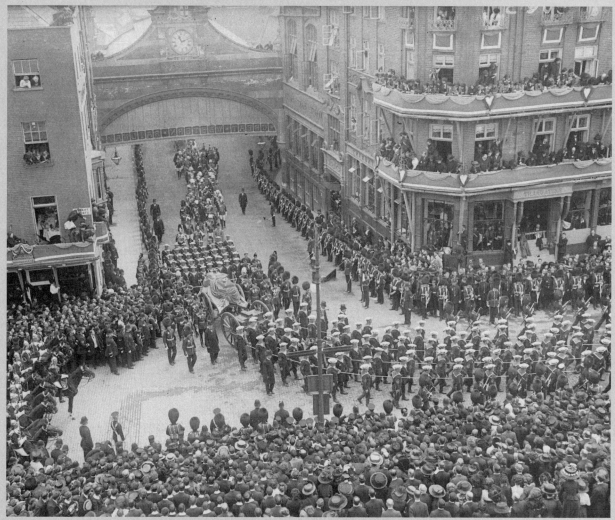

King Edward VII's funeral – the royal procession at Windsor, 1910.

The Duke of Connaught, Queen Victoria's son, with the Governor of Sierra Leone, 1910.

The 'unsinkable' four-funnelled ship SS *Titanic*, 1910, two years before her tragic icy demise off Newfoundland.

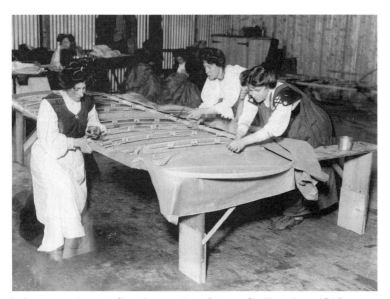

Women workers at Short's aeroplane factory, Shellbeach, c. 1910.

David Lloyd George (left) and Winston Churchill in central London.

A British Army aeroplane of 1910.

Keir Hardie, the first parliamentary leader of the Labour Party, making a speech in London's Trafalgar Square in 1910.

Robert Falcon Scott, who captained the ill-fated British expedition to Antarctica, boarding the *Terra Nova*, June 1910.

Dr Hawley Crippen (right) leaving the liner *Montrose* escorted by Inspector Drew, after being arrested at sea in November 1910 for the murder of his wife, Belle Elmore.

Gipsy children running beside the royal carriage during King George V's visit to Epsom races, 1911.

Early cost-cutting exercise in London: a camel is put to use mowing the lawns in 1911.

City of London police testing stands before the 1913 coronation.

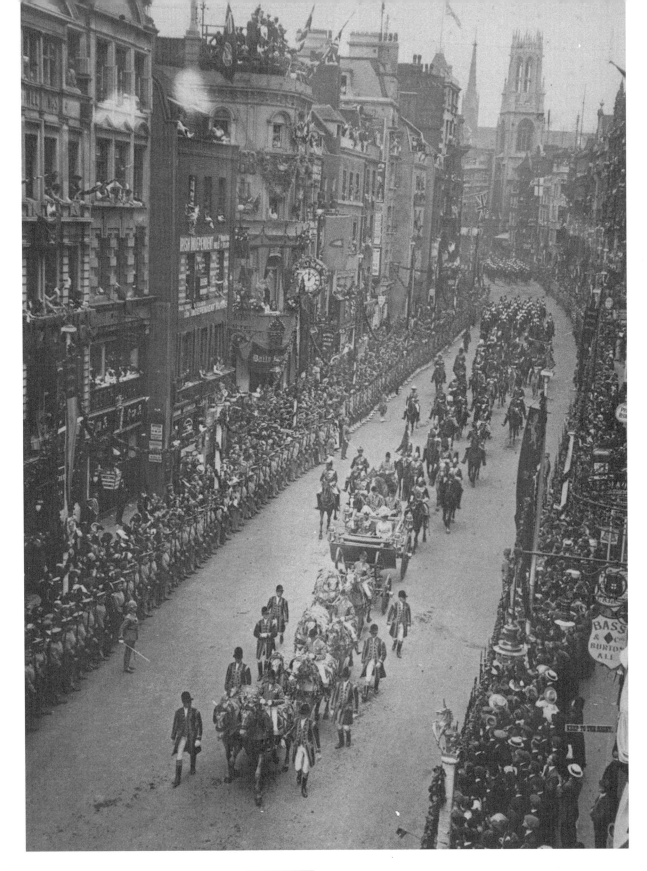

Facing page: The coronation progression of King George V and Queen Mary through Fleet Street, London, June 1911.

King George V having lunch in the jungle in Nepal, 1912.

Members of the Royal Army Medical Corps working with the British wounded in France, 1916, in the First World War.

Above left: Charlie Chaplin starring in his film *Shoulder Arms*, 1918.

King George V and Queen Mary on their royal silver wedding day at Buckingham Palace, July 1919.

Garden party at Buckingham Palace: women police assembled at the Duke of York steps in central London, 1919.

Film stars Miss Mary Pickford and
her second husband, Douglas
Fairbanks Sen., on arrival at
Southampton from the United
States, 1920.

Sir Arthur Conan Doyle, famous for creating the fictional London detective Sherlock Holmes, strkes a pose in 1921.

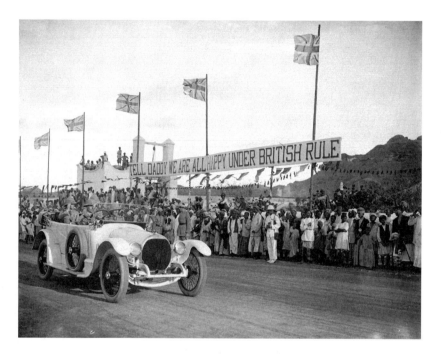

The Prince of Wales in Aden in 1921, passing locals and a decorative announcement: TELL DADDY WE ARE ALL HAPPY UNDER BRITISH RULE. 'Daddy' is King George V.

The Prince of Wales during his 1922 tour to Japan and the East: here, at Sarkai Shiga, he receives a gift of sheep presented by the Maliks of the Khyber Agency.

Artist Jacob Epstein with one of his sculptures, March 1922.

The Queen Mother and her husband King George VI enjoy a game of golf while on their honeymoon, 1922.

A general view of Queen Alexandra's funeral cortège and the royal mourners leaving Sandringham, 1925.

Passengers rush for trams on the Victoria Embankment, London, during a rail strike.

The general public holidaying by the seaside in the Easter sunshine at Eastbourne, Sussex, 1926.

American golfer Bobby Jones teeing off at Sunningdale, June 1926.

T.E. Lawrence 'of Arabia' caught on film, 1927, during his service in the RAF. Eight years later he died in a motorcycling accident in Dorset.

King George V shooting at Sandringham, 1928.

The Duchess of York at a ceremony during which she presented a shamrock to the Irish Guards, 1928.

The Queen and the Duchess of York pictured in March 1928 at a Civil Service art exhibition.

A busy Covent Garden scene, London, May 1929.

The Graf Zeppelin airship flying over a section of the FA Cup final crowd at Wembley Stadium in 1930. On the pitch, Arsenal beat Huddersfield Town 2–0.

H.G. Wells, pioneer of English science fiction, frozen in time in November 1931.

Below: A contrast in clothing during the great heatwave of 1933.

Princess Elizabeth riding her favourite pony in Windsor Great Park on her seventh birthday, April 1933.

Cunard–White Star liner *Queen Mary* leaves Southampton on her maiden voyage to New York, 1936.

Queen Elizabeth with her husband, King George VI, and their daughters Elizabeth and Margaret. The picture was taken after the coronation of her husband in 1937 following the abdication of his brother, Edward VIII.

Top right: The Duke (formerly King Edward VIII) and Duchess of Windsor at their controversial meeting with German leader Adolf Hitler in Munich on 22 October 1937.

Middle right: King George VI and Queen Elizabeth leave the government building after opening the Empire Exhibition from a dais in Bellahouston Park, Glasgow, May 1938.

Two policemen on the streets of London, both equipped with gas masks at the start of the Second World War, September 1939.

Workers fill the streets of London with sandbags during the early days of the Second World War.

Below left: London evacuees, complete with gas masks and luggage, all set for their move to the country after the outbreak of war.

Observation post at the Savoy, London, in 1939. It consisted of a reinforced concrete pill-box, equipped with radio and special telephones, and was manned by ARP wardens from the hotel's staff.

Princess Elizabeth (behind) and Princess Margaret with their nurse Marion Crawford on a trip down the river, 1940.

Damaged caused to London's buildings and houses from an air raid during the Blitz, 1940.

A fireman enjoys a refreshing drink in the central London area as he works to clear rubble caused by bombing in the Blitz.

Princess Elizabeth and Princess Margaret in the country, where they stayed during the Second World War. In view of the need for saving petrol, their pony-cart was brought into use.

A lamplighter doing his rounds on a foggy day in Blackfriars, London.

Top: Young London residents celebrate VE-Day (marking the Allied victory over Germany and an end to the Second World War in Europe) amid the ruins of their home in Battersea, May 1945.

Princess Elizabeth in 1947, on the occasion when she received the Freedom of the City of London. It was the first significant ceremony which the princess attended unaccompanied.

Right: Prime Minister Clement Attlee is leaving 10 Downing Street in August 1947 on his way to the House of Commons, to deliver his crisis speech and present Britain's austerity programme for the next twelve months.

The blocked Gravesend–Meopham road, with snowdrifts of up to four feet deep, winter 1947.

On display at St James's Palace are the many wedding gifts given to the future Queen after she married the Duke of Edinburgh in 1947.

Princess Elizabeth (now Queen Elizabeth II) and Lieutenant Philip Mountbatten (now the Duke of Edinburgh) leaving Westminster Abbey in London after their wedding ceremony, November 1947.

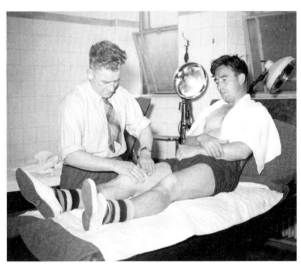

Denis Compton, England and Middlesex cricketer and Arsenal footballer, is massaged by trainer Jack Milne at Highbury Stadium, 1947.

Jamaican immigrants welcomed by RAF officials from the Colonial Office in 1948 after the ex-troopship *Empire Windrush* landed them at Tilbury.

First babies born on the NHS under the new Health Act, July 1948.

The *Queen Elizabeth* sails from Southampton, December 1948, after being held up by a strike and then fog.

A crowd gathering outside Wandsworth Prison, London, in August 1949, after the execution of John George Haigh (for the murder of Mrs Olivia Durand-Deacon, whose body had been destroyed in an acid bath).

General view of the official signing ceremony creating the North Atlantic Treaty Organisation (NATO) in Washington, April 1948.

Film stars Stewart Granger and Jean Simmons at Harringay Arena, London, 1949: they saw Dave Sands of Australia score a one-round victory over Britain's Dick Turpin, the holder, for the British Empire middleweight championship.

Volunteers filling sandbags to seal off a fire at Creswell Colliery near Worksop, Nottinghamshire, where 80 miners lost their lives in the colliery's underground workings in September 1950. About a hundred men escaped to safety.

Prince Charles (now Prince of Wales) with his mother Princess Elizabeth (now the Queen) on arrival in Scotland for their trip to Balmoral, 1950.

Far right: Prince Charles on his third birthday having a morning pram ride through St James's Park in London, November 1951.

Mr P. Sharp, a boilermaker, takes his seat within the hollow, streamlined propeller cone to eat in the warmth, during the annual overhaul of the liner *Queen Mary* at Southampton, November 1951.

February 1952: through sombre crowds lining sodden streets, King George VI comes back to his capital from Sandringham to lie in state in Westminster Hall until his funeral. The draped coffin is carried from the train at King's Cross Station in London. On the coffin rest a wreath from the widowed Queen Mother and the Imperial State Crown.

Rescue workers searching through the wreckage for dead and injured passengers after an express train hit the rear of a local train at Harrow and Wealdstone Station in Middlesex, October 1952.

Far left: Peter Wooldridge Townsend, the man Princess Margaret could not marry.

On their regular parade in a gaggle through the streets of Lacock – the National Trust village in Wiltshire – local geese go in search of titbits.

Members of the public are helped by firemen pulling a small boat in flood-stricken Canvey Island, Essex, February 1953.

A policeman in the garden of 10 Rillington Place in Notting Hill, London, where police found human bones buried a few inches under the soil. They had been burnt in an attempt to destroy them. The bodies of four strangled women had already been discovered at the address.

John Christie is helped, hooded, from a Black Maria. He was charged by police with three murders in the Rillington Place case, April 1953.

Queen Elizabeth II at her coronation in Westminster Abbey, London, June 1953.

Facing page top left: Edmund Hillary (right) from New Zealand and Sherpa Tensing Norgay, after arriving at Heathrow Airport in July 1953 following their successful ascent of Mount Everest, with Colonel John Hunt (left), the expedition leader.

Facing page top right: The Duke and Duchess of Windsor on the liner *United States*, in December 1954, travelling to spend Christmas with friends in America.

Facing page bottom: Prince Charles with the Queen and his sister Princess Anne at the Royal Windsor Horse Show, May 1955.

Mrs Violet van der Elst, for years an active campaigner against capital punishment, stands apart from police officers outside Holloway Prison, in north London, as Ruth Ellis (the last woman to receive the death penalty in Great Britain) is executed on 13 July 1955.

Below left: Labour leader Clement Attlee addresses the 1955 party conference at Margate.

Sir Winston and Lady Churchill pictured on his 80th birthday, November 1955.

Prime Minister Sir Anthony Eden leaving 10 Downing Street on his way to the House of Commons, November 1956.

Below left: Children selected by the Overseas League in 1957 to become permanent settlers in New Zealand. Pictured are Janet and Claudia Lowe from Hounslow, Middlesex

Prince Charles and sister Princess Anne, watched closely by the Queen, the Duke of Edinburgh and a corgi, play on a seesaw while visiting a sawmill on the Balmoral estate, Scotland, during their holiday in 1957.

Between the severed tail and a twisted propeller, searchers hunt for bodies amid the wreckage of the Aquila Airways double-deck flying-boat which crashed on the slopes of a chalk pit on the Isle of Wight and burst into flames, November 1957.

Mourners stand in silence as the coffin of Roger Byrne, Manchester United's captain, is borne from Flixton Parish Church, near Manchester, for the last journey to the crematorium. Byrne was one of the United players killed in the 1958 air crash at Munich.

Shopkeepers bail out water from their flooded premises in Chelmsford, Essex. The town was one of the worst affected by a great storm in September 1958.

Prime Minister Harold Macmillan's car leads the first vehicles along Britain's first motorway, the eight-mile-long Preston Bypass, at the end of 1958.

The prototype of the all-British SR N1 hovercraft, designed by Christopher Cockerell, during a demonstration at Cowes on the Isle of Wight, June 1959.

Margaret Thatcher, Conservative candidate for Finchley, is introduced to darts in a local pub by greengrocer Fred Booth in September 1959. Mrs Thatcher became the first woman barrister to be an MP.

Aneurin Bevan speaking at the Labour Party Special Conference in Blackpool, 1959.

The busy scene in January 1962 as smallpox vaccinations are given in a special clinic at St George's Hall, Bradford, after four people were found to have the disease locally.

Prime Minister Harold Macmillan (right) points out the lie of the land at Birch Grove, his Sussex home, to visiting US President John F. Kennedy during a break in their informal talks, June 1963.

Linslade, Buckinghamshire, August 1963: under the guidance of police officers, three hooded men are taken to waiting police cars at after being remanded in custody on charges in connection with the great train robbery the previous week. Two women were also remanded in custody.

Alec Issigonis, creator of the British Motor Corporation Mini car range, drives the one millionth Mini off the production line at Austin's Longbridge Works in Birmingham, February 1965.

Harold Wilson relaxing with his wife and son on the uninhabited Samson Island, Isles of Scilly, on holiday from the cares of prime ministership.

The scene at Aberfan, Glamorgan, in October 1966 after a man-made mountain of pit waste slid down onto Pantglas School and a row of housing, killing 116 children and 28 adults.

The moment immediately before the disaster as *Bluebird* streaks across on Coniston Water, Lancashire, in January 1967. A second later, the boat somersaulted into the air before sinking in a smother of spray and foaming water. Donald Campbell met his death inside as he reached a speed of 300 miles per hour.

The oil-soiled sea continues its relentless battering of the tanker *Torrey Canyon*, which has broken in two on the Seven Stones Reef off Land's End, March 1967.

The collapsed upper corner of a 22-storey block of flats in Canning Town, beside West Ham greyhound stadium in London's East End, May 1968. An early morning explosion left three people dead and 80 families homeless.

Twisted rails point to a derailed coach of the 2.45 p.m. Paignton–Paddington express after the rear four coaches of the train had left the track at Skeel Bridge, Somerset in June 1969. Twenty-eight people were injured, eight seriously.

The Prince of Wales' investiture at Caernarvon Castle, July 1969.

'Alive, alive-o!' they sing. Harold Wilson joins actress Violet Carson – Ena Sharples of *Coronation Street* – in a duet at the Royal Lancaster Hotel in London. The Prime Minister was presenting the 1970 *Sun* TV awards.

Rear Admiral Morgan Giles, Conservative candidate for Winchester, climbs a political ladder to the thatched roof of a 300-year-old cottage in the village of Micheldever for some electoral canvassing, June 1970.

The British-assembled pre-production Concorde 01 taking to the air from Filton, December 1971. But the maiden flight was cut short when warning lights came on, triggered by some undercarriage problems.

Party leader Jeremy Thorpe at the 1972 Liberal Assembly in Margate.

Princess Anne and Captain Mark Phillips appear on the balcony of Buckingham Palace on their wedding day, November 1973.

Below left: Tory rebel Enoch Powell in 1974 during a Common Market speech he delivered to the packed Victoria Hall, Shipley.

Below right: A large caricature head of Prime Minister Edward Heath and anti-Heath posters among the crowd in Downing Street as they wait for some sign of a break in the election deadlock, 1974.

Screaming Lord Sutch, leader of the Monster Raving Loony Party, with party chairman Douglas Mew, hands in a protest petition to the Prime Minister at 10 Downing Street, October 1974.

Peace campaigners and joint winners of the 1976 Nobel Peace Prize, Mairead Corrigan (left) and Mrs Betty Williams, among 10,000 Catholic and Protestant women during a peace demonstration in Republican areas of Belfast.

Facing page top: Staines Reservoir, Middlesex, during the drought of 1976.

Facing page bottom: Freddie Laker at Gatwick Airport in September 1976 for the inaugural flight of his airline's Skytrain service to America, which operated until the company's demise in February 1982.

Left: William Hague, aged 16, gets down to some serious study on his return to Wath Comprehensive School, near Rotherham, after astonishing delegates at the 1977 Tory conference in Blackpool with a polished, fluent speech during the debate on economic policy. He was rewarded with cheers from Margaret Thatcher and a standing ovation.

An unpleasant official rubbish dump in Leicester Square, February 1979, on the day that orders went out to Westminster City Council's cleansing chief to close the 34 official dumps with 'whatever labour he can find'.

Bottom left: Margaret Thatcher waves victoriously from the doorstep of 10 Downing Street after the 1979 general election.

Anthony Blunt, addressing a press conference at the *Times* newspaper officer in London after his sensational disclosure that he is a Russian spy.

The 3,500-ton Greek cargo ship *Athena B*, which was blown ashore on Brighton beach in a gale, January 1980.

Police officers eat lunch as they take a break from coping with a mass picket of the privately owned steelworks at Sheerness.

Camilla Parker-Bowles and the future Princess Diana at Ludlow racecourse, October 1980, to watch the Irish gelding Allibar which Prince Charles was riding in the amateur riders' handicap steeplechase (he finished second).

A youth displays the swastika, symbol of Nazi Germany, patterned on his T-shirt during a 1980 British movement march from Hyde Park to Paddington Recreation Ground, London. The movement had grown to a total membership of more than 3,000 during the previous two years, benefiting from the recent disintegration of the National Front into squabbling splinter groups.

The 'Yorkshire Ripper', Bradford lorry driver Peter Sutcliffe (under cover of a blanket), at Dewsbury Magistrates Court, after he was committed in custody to stand trial at Leeds Crown Court in February 1981, charged with the murder of 13 women and the attempted murder of seven others.

The Prince of Wales and his fiancée Lady Diana Spencer arriving at the Goldsmiths Hall in London for an entertainment in aid of the Royal Opera House development appeal, March 1981.

A police car blazes at the corner of Atlantic Road and Brixton Road, Brixton, south London, in a fresh outbreak of the street violence of 1981.

The newly married Prince and Princess of Wales wave to the crowds as they are taken to Buckingham Palace after their wedding ceremony at St Paul's Cathedral, July 1981.

American car chief John De Lorean at the wheel of his company's sports car on press review day of Motorfair, the London Motor Show, 1981.

GLC Transport Committee chairman Dave Wetzel (left) and GLC leader Ken Livingstone in February 1982, launching a publicity campaign at County Hall, London, against the Law Lords' verdict abolishing cheap London Transport fees.

Below left: Pope John Paul II kisses the ground in a traditional gesture after leaving the plane which brought him to Gatwick at the start of his historic six-day pastoral visit to Britain in 1982.

Below right: The Queen with her guest, American President Ronald Reagan, as they ride in Windsor Home Park, 1982.

The scene of terrorist bomb devastation at the Droppin Well pub-disco in Ballykelly, Londonderry, Northern Ireland, in December 1982. Seventeen people lost their lives, including eight soldiers.

Above right: Seasoned anti-hunt campaigner, pacifist and Methodist preacher the Rev. Lord Soper in 1983, preaching at Speaker's Corner in London's Hyde Park – a tradition which he continued until 1981, the year he died.

The house of murderer Dennis Nilsen in Muswell Hill, London. Police are digging for the remains of human bodies after pieces of human flesh were found to be blocking a drain outside the house when a plumber called to clear it, February 1981.

Labour leader Neil Kinnock and his wife Glenys dodge the waves on Brighton beach at party conference time, 1983.

Polaris submarine at the Hayward Gallery, South Bank, London, being constructed from 5,000 second-hand tyres. The work of Scots-born sculptor David Mach, it was the largest exhibit in the Arts Council's 1983 sculpture show.

Far right: Prince Edward in a determined pose during rehearsals for Arthur Miller's play *The Crucible* at Jesus College, Cambridge, November 1983.

Assistance for a victim of the IRA Harrods bomb blast, at Westminster Hospital. The lunchtime explosion, which happened at the Knightsbridge department store just before Christmas 1983, killed six people and injured many more.

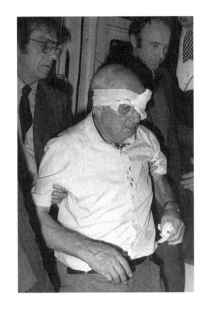

The coffin of WPC Yvonne Fletcher is borne into Salisbury Cathedral, following her murder outside the Libyan People's Bureau in London during the siege there in 1984.

A cheeky picket calmly 'inspects' a line of linked policemen outside the Orgreave coking plant in Yorkshire, during the 1984 miners' dispute.

The shattered top four floors of Brighton's Grand Hotel, devastated by an IRA bomb which left five people dead and 31 injured. The bomb exploded behind bathroom panelling in room 629 and was aimed at delegates attending the 1984 Conservative Party Conference.

Deals on Wheels, January 1985: Nicholas Pearce, managing director of Cellular One, speaking directly to the USA while cycling through London traffic with the first truly portable telephone.

Sir Clive Sinclair demonstrates his current transport idea – the C5 electric vehicle – at Alexandra Palace, London early in 1985.

Emergency services attend to the smoking fuselage of a British Airtours Boeing 737 which was engulfed by fire on the runway of Manchester Airport in August 1985. The plane was taxi-ing on the runway before take-off when an explosion in an engine was followed by fire, trapping 137 people on board. Fifty-five people were killed in the tragedy.

Paddy Ashdown speaking at a Liberal CND meeting, 1985.

The founders of the Social Democratic Party in Bath, January 1986, on the eve of the fifth anniversary of the party's launch. From left: Shirley Williams (SDP president), David Owen (SDP leader), Roy Jenkins and Bill Rogers.

Pickets clash with police during a night vigil outside Rupert Murdoch's hi-tech print plant in Wapping, London, as the print unions' dispute with News International goes on.

The Duke of York seals his marriage to Sarah Ferguson with a kiss on the balcony of Buckingham Palace, July 1986. Prince Edward stands to the right of the couple.

A massive shark appears to have nose-dived into a pretty row of terraced cottages at Headington, Oxfordshire in 1986. The real story was that cinema manager Bill Heine hired a crane to lower the 25-foot glass-fibre fish, sculpted by John Buckley, on to his roof to mark the anniversary of the Nagasaki A-bomb (9 August).

The slow, steady winching operation to raise the capsized ferry *Herald of Free Enterprise* continues at Zeebrugge in Belgium, April 1987. After five hours, most of the superstructure was clearly visible.

Prime Minister Margaret Thatcher and party chairman Norman Tebbit wave to supporters as the Conservatives celebrate being elected for a third time, June 1987.

The hearse bearing Marie Wilson's coffin passes the scene of the IRA bomb explosion in which she died, at Enniskillen, Northern Ireland on Remembrance Sunday 1987.

The top of the fire-damaged escalators at King's Cross underground station, London, after a huge blaze in November 1987.

Below left: Jill Morrell lights a candle for her boyfriend, the journalist John McCarthy who had been kidnapped in Beirut, during a vigil at St Bride's Church in Fleet Street, London, on New Year's Eve 1987.

Below right: TV personality Jill Dando pictured in 1988.

Piper Alpha oil platform on fire in the North Sea, July 1988.

Facing page top: The scene near London's Clapham Junction station following the rail crash in which 35 people died. At 8.13 a.m. on Monday, 12 December 1988, a London-bound commuter train ploughed into a stationary train there.

Facing page bottom: The wrecked nose section of the Pan Am Boeing 747 which crashed in a field near Lockerbie, Dumfries in December 1988, after a terrorist bomb had gone off in the aircraft's hold.

Junior health minister Edwina Currie holding political hot potatoes in February 1989, having whipped up controversy with remarks about salmonella in British eggs.

Above right: Over 5,000 Moslem marchers parade through Leicester to protest about Salman Rushdie's book, *The Satanic Verses,* following the proclamation of a *fatwa* against the author by Ayatollah Khomeini of Iran in 1989.

Stepping out from an East London tube station after their 'passing-out' parade are four members of the London Chapter of the New York-style Guardian Angels, May 1989.

The wrecked hull of the *Marchioness* lies partially submerged in shallow water on the north bank of the River Thames, just south of Southwark Bridge, where she was hit by the dredger *Bowbelle.*

The final underground section between the Kent coast and the terminal site has just been broken through in the Channel Tunnel. The workers are celebrating their arrival in Folkestone, November 1990.

Margaret Thatcher with her husband Denis leaving
10 Downing Street for the last time, November 1990.

The Prince of Wales (dark shirt) and Major James Hewitt
in action during a polo match at the Royal Berkshire Polo
Club, 1991.

A policewoman wears a protective mask as she directs
traffic in fumy Central London, September 1991.

Controversial in life and death: Robert Maxwell, the
chairman of Mirror Group Newspapers, in November
1991, shortly before he mysteriously died at sea.

Released Middle East hostage Terry Waite shares a joke with Archbishop of Canterbury Robert Runcie at RAF Lyneham, November 1991.

Wheeler-peelers PC Dave Murphy (left) and PC Jason Smith test ride their new mountain bikes, purchased by Tottenham police to keep up with local cycle-related crime, 1991.

Freemasons put on their regalia at Earls court, June 1992, for the 275th anniversary of the foundation of the premier Grand Lodge.

Facing page: The full extent is seen of the damage from the fire that swept through St George's Hall at Windsor Castle in 1992.

Edinburgh's Palace of Holyroodhouse floodlit, for the first time, to mark the 1992 European heads of state meeting there.

Commander Tim Laurence and Princess Anne after their wedding at Crathie Church, Balmoral, in December 1992.

The stricken oil tanker *Braer*, which went aground off the Shetland coast, January 1993.

Denise Bulger hangs her head at the funeral, in Merseyside, of her two-year-old son James, whose death early in 1993 at the hands of two local youngsters shocked the nation.

The Prince and Princess of Wales at a banquet in the Portuguese embassy, London, April 1993.

The dramatic scene at Holbeck Hotel, Scarborough, after a massive landslip, 1993.

Rupert Murdoch speaking in September 1993 at the launch of Sky Television's new multi-channel package in London, giving viewers a choice of more than 20 channels.

The demolition of two 19-storey blocks of flats at Queen Elizabeth Square, Gorbals, Glasgow, in September 1993 was billed as the biggest controlled explosion in Europe since the Second World War.

Hugh Grant, star of 1994 box office hit *Four Weddings and a Funeral*, arrives for the film's charity première with his girlfriend, actress and Estée Lauder model Elizabeth Hurley, at the Odeon cinema in London's Leicester Square.

TV presenter Anneka Rice and National Lottery chairman Sir Ron Dearing hit the red start button to launch the National Lottery, November 1994.

Frantic bidding in early 1995 on the floor of the London International Financial Futures and Options Exchange.

Barings Bank fugitive trader Nick Leeson is escorted by police officers at Frankfurt Airport, March 1995, following his arrival from Malaysia. Leeson was held responsible for the collapse of Barings Merchant Bank with the loss of millions of dollars.

The Queen, Queen Mother and Princess Margaret watch a procession of vintage planes fly over Buckingham Palace. The flypast was held as part of national celebrations to commemorate the 50th anniversary of VE-Day, May 1995.

Left to right: Party leaders John Major (Conservative), Paddy Ashdown (Liberal Democrats) and Tony Blair (Labour) talk before a Beating the Retreat ceremony in London, during the VJ-Day commemorations, 1995.

At Eton College, Prince William signs the traditional entrance book watched by his parents, the Prince and Princess of Wales, and younger brother Prince Harry, August 1995.

BRITAIN'S CENTURY

Facing page: A young French girl finds her path to the Channel blocked by the Stena Sealink *Challenger* ferry, which ran aground just outside Calais.

Labour leader Tony Blair (right) takes part in a ball-heading contest with Newcastle United boss Kevin Keegan in Brighton during a break in the playground during Labour's 1995 party conference.

The mangled remains of a bus blown apart by an IRA bomb in Aldwych, London, in February 1996.

Princess Diana in front of the Taj Mahal during a royal tour of India, 1996

Above right: Diana, Princess of Wales leaves the studios of the English National Ballet following a lunch on the day in August 1996 that her marriage to the Prince of Wales officially came to an end with the issue of the decree absolute.

Prime Minister Tony Blair surrounded by his 'babes', the 101 female Labour MPs at Westminster, after their party's victory in the 1997 general election.

Paulette Dubois, a music student from Edinburgh, gets into the spirit of the 26th annual Gay Pride Festival parade in London, July 1997.

Facing page bottom: Seventeen candles of remembrance are lit at Dunblane Cathedral in October 1996 for a memorial service for the 16 children and teacher who died in the Dunblane Primary School shooting the previous March.

The Prince of Wales with sons Prince William and Prince Harry above the Falls of Muick, during their traditional Balmoral summer holiday, 1997.

Alone with his thoughts, Earl Spencer lays flowers on the island in the grounds of the Spencer family home at Althorp, Northamptonshire, where his sister Diana, Princess of Wales, lies buried.

Facing page: The coffin of Diana, Princess of Wales is carried from Westminster Abbey following her funeral service, September 1997.

Harrods boss Mohammed Al Fayed pictured in January 1998 at what looks like a crowning moment.

Top left: David Trimble, leader of the Ulster Unionist Party, at a news conference in the Unionist Belfast offices, June 1998.

Middle left: Members of the Portadown Lodge of the Orange Order in Northern Ireland are stopped by a roadblock on leaving Drumcree Church, preventing them completing the traditional route of the annual march down the nationalist Garvaghy Road, July 1998.

Left to right: Prime Minister Tony Blair, deputy Labour Party leader John Prescott and Chancellor of the Exchequer Gordon Brown listen intently to a speech at the 1998 Labour party conference, Blackpool.

Fireworks explode over the Albert Memorial (in London's Hyde Park) which was officially reopened in October 1998 by the Queen, marking the end of a four-year restoration project.

Top right: Prince Edward with his new bride-to-be Sophie Rhys-Jones at St James's Palace, London, February 1999.

The Prince of Wales and Camilla Parker-Bowles step out in public together for the first time, following a 50th birthday dinner-dance for Mrs Parker-Bowles' sister at the Ritz Hotel, London, January 1999.

White hope for Cool Britannia, or white elephant? Night scene of the capital's new landmark, the Millennium Dome in Greenwich, south-east London.

Place your cross here . . . A local resident has just cast his vote in Macduff, north-east Scotland, on 6 May 1999, the day of elections for the Scottish Parliament – the first for nearly 300 years.

Braveheart meets sore head: John Orr, in full Highland gear with broadsword, outside a polling station in Edinburgh. Diehard nationalist Orr had planned to be the first person in Scotland to vote in the Scottish elections, but overslept after spending a night out with a pal.